Bishopbriggs
in old picture postcards

by Christine Miller

European Library   ZALTBOMMEL/THE NETHERLANDS

GB ISBN 90 288 6107 6 / CIP

© 1995 European Library – Zaltbommel/The Netherlands

Introduction

The history of the Bishopbriggs area can be traced back to Roman times. On the northern edge of Bishopbriggs Agricola raised forts at Balmuildy and Cadder about 80 AD; these would have been made from local timber from the extensive woodland which covered the area. It would be sixty years on from that time before another General, Lollius Urbicus, rebuilt the forts in stone and connected them and others across the Forth and Clyde Valley with a 'wall' or ditch and rampart, which became known as the Antonine Wall. When the Forth and Clyde Canal was dug through the course of the wall during the 1770s, many Roman artefacts were found. Cadder and Balmuildy Forts were properly excavated in 1929 and 1912 respectively.

The name Bishopbriggs does not date from Roman times; in fact, there is quite a controversy over the origin and development of the name. The oldest documented name of the village is evidently 'Bishop Bridge', which appears in parish records dated 1665. Certainly, the land was given to the Bishop of Glasgow by Malcolm IV in 1159. Some say the place got its proper name from a bridge that spanned the Callie Burn. This same story relates that the unfortunate gentleman who built the bridge had to take refuge for a night under its cold archway, in order to escape from a howling mob of infuriated parishioners. If this were all true, we would have an interesting glimpse of a Reformation riot in the village around 400 years ago.

The history of the area from the Romans until the eighteenth century is very much the history of Cadder. There has been a church on the site at Cadder for more than 800 years. In 1507 the vicarage of Cadder was annexed to the University of Glasgow 'for the advantage of the clergy, and for cherishing varied and superior learning, and the society of learned men therein'. Sir Archibald Calderwood, the vicar of Cadder, bequeathed to the college an annuity of eight shillings for a collection for the dean, regents, professors and students. He further assigned an annual payment of ten shillings to the Curate of Cadder to pray for him daily at mass.

After the Reformation the temporalities came into the possession of two families who again transfered them to the college. In 1821 they were bought up by the heritors and Kirk Session, who then became the patrons of the parish; they included Stirling of Cadder, Christie of Bedlay and Sprot of Garnkirk. Cadder House and the adjoining estate belonged to the family of Stirling. The lands of Cadder, in 1180, were given to the Bishop of Glasgow by King William the Lion, 'for the safety of his soul', and soon afterwards they were feued out to Sir Alexander, Sheriff of Stirling, in whose family they remained for over 700 years. The school at Cadder was set up in the late seventeenth century, many years before the first school in the village of Bishopbriggs. In the eighteenth century Kirkton of Cadder was a self-contained 'fermetoun', although the settlement never really expanded beyond its original boundary. With the development of quarrying and mining in the nineteenth century the community focus moved away from Cadder to the village of Bishopbriggs. The railway, which opened in 1842, gave an added impetus to this development. However, the village never developed at a huge pace, and growth was slow until the 1930s and 1950s. From 1861 to 1901 the population only increased by about 100 every ten years.

During the late nineteenth century the Carron Company was the main employer and gave work to many residents and others in the surrounding area. The company built a large number of workers' houses in Mavis Valley and Jellyhill, about a mile from the centre of the village. By the time of the Cadder Pit Disaster in 1913, when twenty-two men died, the mines were past their peak. During the 1920s there were many closures. Most of the quarries were worked out by the turn of the century. In their heyday they had provided sandstone for many of Glasgow's buildings. Afterwards the abandoned quarries became environmental hazards, until most of them were filled in; however, the incidence of building subsidence in southern Bishopbriggs is due to these huge workings.

Manufacturing industry did not make an impact on Bishopbriggs until after the First World War. New developments included engineering firms, brickworks, a wire rope factory, concrete pipe makers and book publishers. Until the 1950s agriculture continued to play an important part in the life of the community, and the farmers always had a ready market for their produce in Glasgow. When the housing boom of the 1950s got under way many of the farms began to disappear. Transport to and from Bishopbriggs was enhanced by the extension of the Glasgow tramway network to Bishopbriggs Cross in 1903. Afterwards a number of wealthy Springburn residents built villas on Kirkintilloch Road and at nearby Brackenbrae. Travelling further afield to Kirkintilloch and beyond remained difficult until the introduction of a motor bus service in the 1920s.

In the early years of the century Bishopbriggs and Cadder became a tourist destination of sorts. The canal steamers brought many day trippers to the leafy glades of Cadder and the trams brought many hikers in search of the countryside and hills. From 1930 Bishopbriggs lay in the administrative area of Lanarkshire County Council's Ninth District and the village became the centre of district affairs. During the 1930s a number of houses were built in the Kenmure and Cadder areas, mainly of the bungalow type. The County Council also built many houses, 356 in Bishopbriggs and 334 in Auchinairn, between 1918 and 1952.

An organisation that went on to play an important part in the modern history of the town, The Bishopbriggs, Auchinairn, Cadder and District Ratepayers Association, was formed shortly after the end of the Second World War. It was instrumental in the campaign to obtain Burgh status for the town, which was granted on 16 May 1964. During this period Bishopbriggs developed from a village into a fair-sized town. The extensive housebuilding of the 1950s and 1960s was largely responsible for this change. Most of the houses in the Balmuildy and Woodhill areas were built on farmland, which led to the disappearance of the rural side of village life familiar to many of the older residents. By 1960 a large part of the Balmuildy area had been built up, and a few years later houses were being erected on the Woodhill Estate. This activity led to a large increase in population, from 11,650 in 1951 to 21,684 in 1971. New schools appeared in the 1960s to serve these estates.

The major highlight of the Burgh years was the opening of Bishopbriggs Sports Centre, in Balmuildy Road, on 12 July 1973. During these years the town must have seemed in danger of becoming a huge housing estate; fortunately this expansion was matched by a similar development in amenity and industry. New schools, churches, shops and restaurants were opened. The industrial estate at Low Moss was set up in 1967 and attracted such well-known names as Collins Publishers, Marley Tiles, B.P. and Wimpey Construction. Further changes came to Bishopbriggs in the early 1970s with the proposed plan, under local government reorganisation, to include the town in the new 'Glasgow District'. An action committee was set up and won the fight to keep Bishopbriggs out of Glasgow; consequently the town joined with Kirkintilloch, Lennoxtown, Moodiesburn, Stepps and Chryston to form the new Strathkelvin District on 16 May 1975. Now that Bishopbriggs has reached a population of about 24,000 there is considerable pressure from interested parties to keep the town within its present dimensions; any further expansion would encroach on the 'green belt' and stretch the local facilities still further. The feeling now in the Community is very much one of consolidation and enhancement of the existing area.

The last ten years have witnessed the most substantial changes to the town since the 1950s. The first major development was the opening of the Triangle Shopping Centre in 1991, which changed the face of the old village at the Cross, and caused the demolition of many of the oldest buildings there. The concerns about losing part of the original village were tempered by the need for more substantial shopping facilities. This had long been a common complaint among local residents. Shortly afterwards, in 1992, the Low Moss Retail Park was opened which brought major stores such as B & Q, Texas, Comet and Curry's to Bishopbriggs. This development necessitated the clearance of much of Low Moss Plantation and the realignment of Kirkintilloch Road. The next major development that awaits Bishopbriggs is the construction of a Relief Road to by-pass the town centre and link with the M80 motorway. This is scheduled to commence in 1997 and will undoubtedly change the face of Bishopbriggs yet again – only for the better we hope!

Due to a shortage of good postcard views and photographs of pre-Second World War Bishopbriggs it has been necessary to include views of Auchinairn, Robroyston and Stobhill. Auchinairn was certainly a separate village with its own, long history, but it does have links with Bishopbriggs, as does Robroyston and Stobhill, so it is quite appropriate to include them here. I would like to thank Strathkelvin District Libraries for the use of their collection to compile this book, and the many local people who contributed prints to the library collection, who are too numerous to mention. I would also like to thank my colleague, Don Martin, for his help and advice in the compilation of this book.

1 This photograph shows an old house at the corner of Schoolfield Lane about 1930. Many new residents of Bishopbriggs will be unfamiliar with the name Schoolfield, which formed part of the original village. The area was once known as Crowhill Bog and was bounded on the north by Callie Burn and on the east by the 'Low Road'. The name appears in documents dating from the seventeenth century and houses existed here at that time. In the corner of the building we can see Shorthouse's General Store, with Mrs. Shorthouse in the doorway. In the background is the school, which is now the public library. The houses were demolished in the 1930s and the site is now part of that occupied by the Triangle Shopping Centre.

2 This row of houses on the Main Road, near the top of Hilton Road, were known as Moss cottages. They were built sometime in the late nineteenth century by the Carron Company for some of their workers in the local mines. The houses took their name from the nearby High and Low Moss plantations, which provided a plentiful supply of peat for fuel in the eighteenth and nineteenth centuries. During the eighteenth century this stretch of road from Bearyards Farm to the Torrance Road, then known as the 'Moss Road', was notorious for robberies and murders. The cottages were finally demolished in the 1960s to make way for new housing and industrial developments.

3 Bishopbriggs School, about 1900. The school was opened in 1896 and a contemporary description of the building was given in the *Kirkintilloch Herald* of 26 August of that year: 'The entrance to the school is at the base of the tower and leads directly into a large central hall, which will be used for drill. To the right and left of the tower there are two rooms for the teachers. The central hall is surrounded by the class rooms, which are seven in number, and capable of giving accommodation for 420 scholars... the tower is supplied with a clock which will strike the hours and half hours, and has four dials; and the top of the tower, as well as the ridges of the roof, are of red tile.' Even in this spacious new school overcrowding soon became a problem, and an annexe was added in 1928. The building is now Bishopbriggs Library.

4　This picture shows the original Bishopbriggs school, or 'Old Stirling School', about 1880. It was originated by the widow of Charles Stirling and was also supported by her brother-in-law, Archibald Stirling of Cadder. This 'infant and sewing school' stood between the new school and the public road. The figure in the foreground may well be the headmistress, Miss Marion Graham, who was a well-known personality in the community. She retired from teaching in 1896 when the new school opened. When overcrowding became severe in the late nineteenth century a new, larger school was built and this building was demolished.

5 Cadder Parish School was set up in 1688, but the buildings we see in this picture were not erected until the late eighteenth and early nineteenth centuries. Before the school was built the community had a schoolmaster, who taught the children in a disused barn in the summer and used whatever pupils' homes were available during the winter. The first part of the school was built sometime between 1780 and 1790; the second part, comprising two classrooms and a kitchen, was built twenty years later, and remained in use until the school closed. As the village of Bishopbriggs grew so the focus of community life moved away from Cadder; nevertheless the school continued with its roll of twenty-three pupils until 1980, when it was closed amid strong protests from the villagers.

CADDER SCHOOL.
SCHOOL HOUSE.

6   This illustration of Cadder House is from a 'Renfield Series' postcard postmarked 29 June 1905. Much of the building dates from the seventeenth century, but the west wing was built in 1816 to the designs of David Hamilton. A charter of the lands exists in favour of Sir Archibald Stirling as far back as the reign of William the Lion, in the twelfth century. Previous to the erection of the mansion, an ancient castle stood near the site, and it is said that on one occasion John Knox dispensed the sacrament there. The house is now a Category 'A'-listed building and is used by Cawder Golf Club as their club house.

CAWDER HOUSE, NEAR BISHOPBRIGGS.

7   Kenmure House was built around 1806 by Charles Stirling to the designs of David Hamilton, the famous Glasgow architect. Mr. Stirling resided there until 1816, when he sold the estate for £40,000 to his elder brother Archibald, afterwards of Keir. Kenmure was occupied by the Stirling family until 1862. The house was set in an attractive estate surrounded by woodland. In the latter part of the nineteenth century the house became a Franciscan convent, as it appears in this photograph. In the early twentieth century various parts of the estate were sold off to build a golf course, a bowling green, an industrial school and private housing. No trace of the house remains.

8　This is a view of Kirkintilloch Road, Bishopbriggs, looking north-west. The street leading up to the right is Brackenbrae Road. Many of the houses in the Brackenbrae area date from the 1930s. There was a set-back in private building during the First World War, but this was reversed in the late 1920s and 1930s. The derelict land in the foreground was the site of underground quarry workings. The other side of the main road was also quarry country, especially around Viewfield Road. The last quarry in that area was infilled in the 1920s. The workings were filled with rubble brought to Duncryne Place by special trams, and when this was completed the area was made into a football pitch.

9   The war memorial was unveiled in 1920 at the corner of Kenmure Avenue. General Archibald Stirling gifted the site for the memorial and a large crowd gathered for the ceremony in November of that year. After the Second World War the names on the memorial included victims of local bombing which occurred on 7 April 1941. On that evening five or six bombs landed on Bishopbriggs near the modern High School. Six local residents died in the incident. The memorial is now incorporated into the Cross Court shopping precinct.

The War Memorial, Bishopbriggs.

10   This is a photograph of Bishopbriggs Fire Brigade taken in March 1927. In 1915 a new fire station was opened in Kirkintilloch Road; previously it had been sited in Crowhill Road. The building was situated on the north side and also incorporated a new police station with housing for the constables and their families. The fire station consisted of a garage, washing space, testing tank and hose drying tower. When the building eventually became outmoded a new station was opened in Hilton Road, in 1973.

11   Bishopbriggs Golf Club House was opened in 1909. The house is situated on the high ground on the left side of Kenmure Avenue. At the time of opening accommodation consisted of a large dining room, a kitchen, a secretary's room, and a club room fitted with 220 boxes, a ladies room fitted with sixty lockers and a greenkeeper's apartment. The total cost of the building was about £1,400. An extension was added in 1971.

GOLF CLUB HOUSE.
BISHOPBRIGGS.

12 This photograph was taken at the opening of Bishopbriggs Golf Course. The construction of a golf course on the Kenmure estate was first discussed in 1905. The club came into being in 1907, but it was not until two years later that the club house was built. The sponsors • planned the club house in the style of a dwelling house, so that it could be sold as such if the club was not a success. During the inter-war years the course became very popular and more recently the club's membership has expanded in parallel with the expansion of the town. In the centre of the photograph is Dr. J.B. Miller, the first club captain.

13   A group of bowlers at Bishopbriggs Green. The bowling green is situated on Kenmure Avenue and was opened in 1906 by Captain Stirling of Keir and Cawder. The green was laid on a portion of Kenmure estate; the entrance was to the left of the avenue leading to Kenmure House. At the time of the opening the pavilion consisted of a clubroom, committee room and toilet, with a store in the basement. The membership roll totalled 104, and the club became the social centre of the village during the summer months. It remains on the original site today and continues to flourish.

14   Huntershill House was built around 1770, and stood just off the old post road to Edinburgh, now called Crowhill Road. Its most famous occupant was Thomas Muir, a son of a wealthy Glasgow merchant, who had acquired Huntershill in 1782. Muir, who was born in 1765, studied and practised law in Glasgow and became a noted Reformer. He was connected with a number of reform societies throughout Scotland, which coincided with revolutionary events in France. Muir was eventually arrested and tried in Edinburgh, where he was found guilty of having created disaffection by means of seditious speeches, and was banished to Botany Bay for fourteen years. In 1796 he escaped and made his way back to France where he died in 1799. The house is now used as a recreation centre.

HUNTERSHILL HOUSE. BISHOPBRIGGS.

15　This photograph shows Carron Company No. 15 pit at Cadder, in 1898, shortly before it opened. A pit-sinking engine is being used to open the shaft, while in the background a new winding engine house is under construction. In the same year several rows of miners' houses were built by the company at Mavis Valley, a short distance from the pit, and in 1903 a further fifty houses were erected for the workers. Although the pit was regarded as one of the best equipped in Scotland it had a short life and was closed in 1923. When in full operation, 600 men were employed underground and on the surface. The closure hit the district badly; only one year previously a large number of workmen's houses had been built in the area.

16 Mavis Valley miners' rows were situated on the north side of the canal, between the towpath and Wilderness Plantation. The houses were built from 1855 onwards and arranged in two rows. The older houses had six privy middens situated at the end of the rows. The newer houses were given one closet to serve four houses. The first one-storey houses contained two rooms, while the one- and two-storey blocks constructed later were of a higher standard. There were washhouses and coal cellars outside the houses.

17   Here we see a typical washday at the rear of the miners' rows in Mavis Valley. The two women in the photograph are Mary Fairbairn (on the left) and Granny Liddell (on the right). Washday took place outside most houses and the water was heated by a coal-fired boiler. The rows consisted of 116 houses situated to the east of No. 17 pit. The site of these houses is now waste ground, although some foundations are still visible to mark the place where families lived and worked.

18   James Neilly and his son, William, lived in cottages at Jellyhill, about 1915. Both men were miners at Cadder Colliery; in mining communities it was common to find father and sons working together in this way. When mining was developed in Cadder during the second half of the nineteenth century, miners' houses were built at Jellyhill as well as Mavis Valley. These were erected on the lands of Jellyhill Farm and the two rows were known as Tar Row, because the roofs were made of tarred felt. There were thirty-two apartment houses with outside water supply. The Tar Row houses were demolished in 1936 after sixty years service. Hilton Terrace now stands on the site.

19　This postcard of No. 17 pit at Cadder was issued at the time of the disaster in 1913. The disaster was caused by a fire at the adjacent No. 15 pit on 3 August 1913. There were twenty-three men trapped underground and only one survided the ordeal. Seven of the victims were from Mavis Valley, the rest from other villages around Bishopbriggs and the north of Glasgow. Some were brothers. From the time the fire was discovered it was eight hours before the nearest rescue brigade was brought from Cowdenbeath, sixty miles away, a fact much lamented in the newspapers of the time. The pit reopened in 1922, but never regained its full operating capacity.

No. 17 Pit Cadder, near Bishopbriggs. Connected with No. 15 Pit by a communicating road through which the survivors & victims were brought to the surface.

20 This postcard was a special edition to commemorate the funeral of the Cadder pit disaster victims. The funeral of the seven local miners took place at Cadder cemetery, a short distance away. The cortege passed along three miles of dusty country roads to the cemetery. At the entrance there now stands a memorial to the victims of the disaster. In the background you can clearly see the miners' rows with the chimney of No. 17 pit in the distance.

Funeral Procession from Mavis Valley to Cadder Cemetery, of 7 victims of the Great Cadder Pit Disaster.

21   Many of the houses in the Brackenbrae area were built in the 1930s. The houses, as shown here, were usually of the bungalow-type popular at that time. Most of the building took place on the lands of Brackenbrae Farm, and Brackenbrae House still stands today amid these modern developments. During the period of largest housing expansion, between 1931 and 1961, the population of Bishopbriggs jumped from 6,658 to 11,604. Also in this picture we can see the original sandstone villas which were built in the village at the turn of the century.

Brackenbrae Avenue, Bishopbriggs.

22 Jimmy Hill, aged sixty-four in 1922, was known as the 'hermit of Pudding Hill'. His 'cave' was actually Springfield Bing, situated about half a mile east of Bishopbriggs. The bing was the remnants of a coal pit in which Jimmy worked in his younger days. The *Kirkintilloch Herald* of 10 May 1922 described how he constructed his unusual home: 'Jimmy dug out the hole with a pick and shovel lent by a miner in the village of Auchinairn. The work of excavation occupied four days, and the fitting of a crude door – evolved from a herring box – and the rough furnishing of the interior did not occupy much time...'

23   This photograph shows the underground workings of Huntershill sandstone quarry, probably around the 1930s. The position of the man at the entrance to the workings gives an idea of the scale of these quarries. In their heyday the quarries at Huntershill, Crowhill and Kenmure provided sandstone for many of Glasgow's largest buildings. Bishopbriggs was indeed 'quarry country' and there were also quarries at Colston, Coltmuir and North Coltpark. The exact date of the opening of Huntershill quarry is difficult to trace; however, it was in existence when the first Ordnance Survey map was produced in 1857.

24   Another view of the underground workings at Huntershill. In the nineteenth century quarrying was one of the main industries in Bishopbriggs, and as with other industries like coalmining it was not always a safe occupation. In 1910 a roof fall at the quarry killed five workers. According to the *Kirkintilloch Herald*, which reported the accident, the quarry 'is worked on the "stoop and room" system that is followed in coal mines. The stone is cut in such a way that pillars are left at intervals to support the roof. A new section of the tunnel was opened about a fortnight ago, and it was in it that the accident happened. Ten men were engaged in the "motion", as the section was technically called and at five o'clock, a short time before the cessation of operations for breakfast, a large portion of the roof, weighing many tons, fell onto the workers.' The huge excavations have rendered much of the Huntershill area prone to subsidence.

25 This is a view of the stepping stones over the River Kelvin, near Bishopbriggs. In the early years of the century the Cadder and Baldernock Parish Councils discussed the possibility of constructing a bridge over this site, since the stones were in need of repair. Although the stones were only usable for a small part of the year, they were a popular crossing point on the Kelvin between Cadder and Balmore, because it saved about half an hour on the usual route. The stones were prone to dislodgement if there were heavy floods – which was very common. In 1927 the popular right-of-way was completely covered with water during the summer and the local newspaper reported that pedestrians crossing the 'steps' resorted to taking off their boots and stockings.

26   This is a photograph of Stobhill Hospital medical and auxiliary staff taken sometime during the First World War. The exterior appearance of the hospital has changed little since its opening in 1904. Improvements have been carried out, and the growth of areas like Bishopbriggs has increased the importance of the hospital. Local people have come to accept the hospital as their own. In recent years, with the current reorganisation of acute health care in Greater Glasgow, there have been fears for the future of the hospital.

27   Patients and staff at Stobhill Hospital celebrating the new year in 1919. With the outbreak of war in 1914 the hospital was requisitioned by the military authorities for the care of wounded servicemen. Existing patients were evacuated to other places, with the exception of the seriously ill, who were accommodated in the infirm blocks. The wounded were brought to a temporary platform next to the old mortuary. As early as September 1914, more than 200 wounded had been admitted to Stobhill, and there was a total bed complement of 1,040 available. At the end of the war, in November 1918, the hospital housed many wounded servicemen and it was not until the end of 1919 that the last of the military staff left.

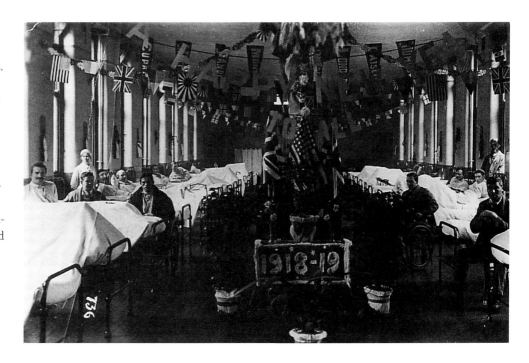

28   Bishopbriggs Station, about 1955. Unfortunately, early illustrations of the station are difficult to find. The railway was important in the development of Bishopbriggs. It opened in 1842, and during the 1850s the first villas were built close to the station, in Springfield Road. The railway company offered free travel to builders in Bishopbriggs, but it was slower to develop than nearby Lenzie. When the station was built there was no footbridge between the platforms as there is today, so passengers had to take a dangerous route across the tracks. The buildings on the left were demolished in the 1960s.

29   This is the bascule bridge which used to span the canal at Cadder. These bridges were at one time universal on the canal, but they were unable to take the weight of modern road transport, and so they were gradually replaced. This bridge has now been superseded by a fixed structure. Otherwise little has changed at this idyllic spot on the canal, although many of the mature trees in the picture have disappeared. Further west the canal crosses the Antonine Wall, and a number of Roman artefacts were discovered when the canal was being constructed and later when Cadder Fort was excavated.

30 The Forth and Clyde Canal was opened in 1790, and was instrumental in changing the face of economic life in central Scotland. The canal also affected life in Bishopbriggs as it passed along the northern edge of the village. One major change was the development of coal-mining in the nineteenth century. Carron Company scows carried ironstone from Cadder Colliery to Carron Iron works near Grangemouth. Coal from the local pits usually went out by rail. On the left of the picture is the bridgekeeper's cottage, which housed the bridgekeeper and the canal banksman. The cottage is now a listed building and is still occupied today. The cottages on the right were known as 'High Row'.

31   This is the bridgekeeper's house at Farm Bridge on the canal. It was located on the north-west corner of the present bridge. The building was also known as 'Brash's' since the Brash family had held the post of bridgekeeper from 1838 to 1942. Adam Brash was the first 'Brash o' the Brig', and kept the job for fifty-seven years. This photograph was taken during John Brash's time in the post, between 1895 and 1928. It is quite possible that he is one of the assembled company in the photograph. The Caledonian Railway Company owned the canal and the bridgekeepers were employed by them. It was their job to keep the canal in proper order, work the locks and bridges and take the tolls for the use of the canal. The cottage was demolished in the 1970s.

32   This postcard shows the S.S. *May Queen* at Cadder. This was, and still is, one of the loveliest spots on the canal. It was a favourite place for passengers on the 'Queen' steamers which sailed the canal between 1893 and 1939. The *May Queen* was built at Kirkintilloch by Peter McGregor and Sons in 1903, and it accommodated 260 passengers. One of the most popular trips on this vessel was the afternoon sailing which included a one-and-a-half hour stop ashore at Cadder. The *May Queen* ceased sailing in 1917.

THE "MAY QUEEN" NEAR CADDER.

33   Here we have another of the 'Queens', the S.S. *Gipsy Queen*, in Cadder woods. The *Gipsy Queen* was launched in 1905 and sailed the canal until 1939. It was the largest boat on the canal and sailed a regular route between Port Dundas and Craigmarloch. From the timetable for 1916 a typical trip was advertised as 'delightful and romantic evening cruises... every Tuesday and Wednesday at 6.30 p.m. – some time at Cadder – music on board'. All this could be had for a return fare of 9d. Cadder was always a popular spot and the guidebook to the route extolled its many virtues: 'As our trig steamer forges its way along the umbrage-shadowed way we seek in vain to penetrate the mass of foliage so as to get a glimpse of Cadder House down in the hollow to the left, but we console ourselves with the delightful coolness of the aquatic avenue, formed by the tall trees on the water's edge.' Who could fail to be tempted by this description!

34 Another view of the *May Queen* at Cadder, coming from the woods. When the ship was launched in 1903 it was intended for cruise parties, picnics, Sunday School trips etc. The cabins, decks, and seatings were made of teak and upholstered with polished pannelling of pine and teak. The steamer was also completely fitted out with electric light. The *May Queen* ended its days as a dispatch boat in connection with Admiralty work.

35   This photograph shows the thatched cottage which stood opposite Cadder Church, until it was burned down in 1928. The building dated from 1628 and was known as Kirkton Cottage. In 1928 the cottage had been unoccupied for some time and the dryness of the roof meant that the fire took hold very quickly. The original Cadder village was known as 'Kirktown of Cadder' in the eighteenth century. At this time slated buildings were unusual in the parish. In 1792 there were only eighteen slated houses, which amounted to only 5 percent of all dwellings in the parish.

36   This scene of the mill at Cadder will be familiar to those who frequent the canal today. However, on closer inspection some features have changed – note the lack of shrubs and vegetation along the canal bank, the open path on the southern edge of the canal, and the bascule bridge. The Mill House still stands on the same site today and dates from around 200 years ago. A previous mill, situated about a quarter of a mile to the west, had been in existence for at least 700 years.

37   This photograph is taken from the wooded area known as the Mill Plantation, and shows the Corn Mill which stood just to the north of the old Mill House. Cadder Mill, previously known as Kirktown Mill, was the property of the Stirling family, owners of Keir and Cawder estates. It was built to serve the farms on the estate. The canal was a major source of water for the mill. The mill was closed sometime between 1924 and 1944.

38 This is an advertisement from the Glasgow Courier of 10 July 1832 regarding the Corn Mill at Cadder. The letting notice gives a clear description of the property and its many attributes. It also indicates that a farm was provided with the mill. This was built in the 1780s, when many farmers were tied to a particular mill, a practice which declined in the nineteenth century.

PARISH OF MEARNS,
REWSHIRE,
SALE.

o sale, by public roup, within
ale Rooms, Queen Street,
day, the 15th day of August

OWNHEAD and PIDMIRE
ssisting of about NINETY-
with the HOUSES, GARDEN

ellent quality, and in good con-
the new line of road from Glas-
are mostly let on lease to a re-
derate rent.
namented with a considerable
and being only an hour's drive
y, are well adapted for Villas.
feus from the Lands, which
village of Newton, are already

e trifling.
he Mansion House, will point
ding purchasers; and further
d on application to James
, No. 86, Miller Street;
bell, writers, Miller Street;
, writers, Ingram Street,
the title deeds and articles of

STUART, Auctioneer.

MILL AND FARMS,
TO LET, ON THE CADDER ESTATE.

To be Let, for such a number of years as may be agreed on, and entered to at Martinmas next, 1832,

THAT Very Superior MEAL MILL at CADDER, lately erected upon the most approved principles, with three pair of Stones, Barley Mill, Pease Pan, &c. &c. in every way complete, with a plentiful supply of Water, and ample accommodation as to Kiln, Lofts and Granaries; situated close upon the banks of the Forth and Clyde Canal, and distant about 4½ miles from Glasgow, by the Kirkintilloch Road. Along with which will be Let, the MILL FARM, containing about 60 Scottish Acres, subdivided into Six Enclosures, with an excellent Dwelling-house and Steading of Offices. The Thrashing Machine goes by water.

The Dwelling-house, Mill and Offices are at present in the natural possession of the proprietor, and may be entered to immediately or at Martinmas next, as may suit intending offerers.

Also, to be Let,

The FARM of LITTLEHILL, containing about 40 Scotish Acres, which is partly enclosed, and to which a field of 9 Acres, at present part of Cadder Mill Farm, will be added, with the privilege of Casting Peats for sale, in Littlehill Moss. A new Dwelling-house will be built on the Farm, and suitable repairs made on the steading.

For conditions of lease and other particulars, apply to John Thoms, factor at Cadder, by Glasgow, who will let the farms so soon as suitable offers are made to him by eligible tenants.

Cadder, 9th July, 1832.

For freight or pas
modation, apply to

Greenock, 9th Jul

Noti
Per BLAND

to forward their Goods
The BLAND will sa
the Lucy at Liverpool,
free of all expense to the
Glasgow, 5th July,

AT L
To sail positively o

FOR B
With leave to deliver a

Apply to
Liverpool,

39   Cadder smiddy (smithy), at the turn of the century. The smiddy was a familiar sight in small villages during the nineteenth and early twentieth centuries, and Cadder was no exception. This particular smiddy was built sometime after 1865, and was situated on Cadder Road, next to the school house. Shoeing horses wasn't only the occupation of the smith. Cartwheels were ringed and farm implements repaired. Someone can be seen in the centre of the photograph attending to a cartwheel. Wheelwrights and blacksmiths worked closely together and often their workshops were situated in close proximity. Remains of the smiddy can still be seen at Cadder today.

40   Another view of Cadder smiddy showing the smith, his assistants and a customer. They are pictured with the tools of their trade, and in the distance an iron tyre for a cart can be seen. The smith was a central figure in the rural community, but by the middle of the twentieth century tractors had largely replaced the horse and there was little traditional work left for the blacksmith.

41 This photograph was taken at Hilton Farm and shows Will Scott with his cart. Hilton Farm is situated on the southern edge of the Wilderness Plantation, near Mavis Valley. The farm first appears in records dating from 1702, and in the first half of this century it was also known as 'Knox's', after the tenant Mr. John Knox, who farmed there for thirty-six years until 1948. The photograph shows a typical horse and cart used for heavy work on the farm. These carts were used extensively on Cadder estate to carry items such as stones, timber and animal fodder.

42   This photograph was taken at Auchinairn Farm and shows Mr. and Mrs. John Letham and family, who farmed the 127 acres at the turn of the century. The farm was situated to the north-east of the village of Old Auchinairn. The farm was demolished in the late 1960s to make way for the housing development on the eastern edge of Bishopbriggs.

43 The village of Auchinairn is situated to the southeast of Bishopbriggs, and nowadays there is no distinct boundary between the two localities. At the turn of the century the situation was very different; between Bishopbriggs and Auchinairn there were the lands of Springfield and East Springfield, as well as some quarries. The population of Auchinairn declined between 1871 and 1891 from 823 to 683, mainly due to the changes in employment patterns. It was a long time before the village spread out from its locus in the Main Street.

44   Auchinairn School was a large two-storey structure with the master's house on the first floor. It was an endowed school with a long history. Rev. James Warden was a native of Auchinairn, and when he died in 1745 he left 100 merks to set up a school in the village. A further bequest from Dr. William Leechman in 1764 secured the future of the project. This far-sighted man stated in the bequest 'that the want of a schoolmaster, house and school at Auchinairn is the cause of many poor children there remaining in obscurity who with proper means of education might be useful to themselves and society'. There was accommodation for 300 children, and in 1891 the roll was 183. The school was demolished in the 1930s.

45　The Wallace Monument at Robroyston was erected in 1900 by public subscription. It was built to mark the site of the house in which William Wallace was betrayed and captured around midnight on 5 August 1305. This building was supposedly demolished in 1822; however, a local antiquarian called Joseph Train, from Kirkintilloch, obtained some of the ceiling timbers. He had the oak rafters made into a chair which he gifted to Sir Walter Scott at Abbotsford. The monument shows the hilt of Wallace's sword in the centre of the cross.

46   This postcard shows Kirkintilloch Road, just north of the cross, around 1905. It is interesting to compare this scene with the road as it today. It is safe to say that there wasn't a traffic problem in 1905! Nowadays this road is jammed with vehicles throughout the day. The tenements on the left side of the road were built in 1898, and the older block on the right dates from the 1880s. In the centre of the picture we can see the wall that bordered Kenmure Estate.

CAWDER ROAD, BISHOPBRIGGS.

47 Another view of Bishopbriggs Cross, taken sometime in the 1930s, showing a much busier scene than the previous picture. The tram terminus can be seen in the centre of the picture. The Springburn Road tram route was extended out to Bishopbriggs in 1903. This was knows as the 'red route', and ran across the city to Rouken Glen. The trams were distinguished by a coloured band which ran around the upper deck. The fare to Glasgow was 2d and the journey took half an hour. Apart from the buildings in the upper right of the picture, which are now replaced by the entrance to the Triangle Shopping Centre, this scene will still be familiar to the residents of Bishopbriggs today. The path at the foot of the picture leads up to the railway station.

48   Another view of Bishopbriggs Cross at the corner of
Kenmure Avenue, which is on
the left. The Commercial Bank
was opened in 1902, shortly
after the tenement block was
built (in 1898). The Royal
Bank of Scotland now occupies this site. The only building that remains on the right
of the picture is that of Quin's
public house. Next to Quin's
there was Tennent's licensed
grocer shop. The population
of Bishopbriggs in 1905 was
1200.

49   This is a more unusual view of Bishopbriggs Cross, taken from the north. On the right of this picture stands Kenmure Cinema, the only cinema in Bishopbriggs. It was opened in 1938 to great applause, since this was regarded as a great benefit to the community. The cinema had capacity to seat one thousand or over. At the opening ceremony Mr. Walker, County Clerk of Lanarkshire, extolled the virtues of the cinema and expressed some views that, are still pertinent today, 'institutions like the cinema were subject to much criticism, and it was said that films were responsible for about half of the divorces, and about three-quarters of the juvenile delinquency... It was one of the greatest aids to temperance, and innocent source of amusement. He refused to admit that it had anything to do with the increase in crime. This is to be blamed on the unsatisfactory economic conditions'. Some things never change! The frontage of the cinema is typical thirties' architecture. On the left are the Schoolfield buildings, which were demolished in the 1930s.

Bishopbriggs from the South.

50   A photograph of the 'Bishop's Bridge'. The remains of a very old bridge can be clearly seen in the culvert that carries the main road across the Bishop's Burn (more usually known as the Callie Burn), near St. Matthew's Church. It is difficult to trace the origins of Bishopbriggs, but this is the site of the original 'Bishop's Bridge', which probably gave the village its name. Certainly there would have been a bridge on this site to carry the Inchbelly Turnpike (the Low Road) over the burn. The origins of the village and its name have caused many arguments over the years.

51   This is a photograph of No. 16 Kirkintilloch Road, sometime in the 1920s. Many sandstone villas were built along the Main Road during the first decade of this century by residents of Colston, Bishopbriggs and Springburn. This mini building boom extended the area of the village and signalled the development of Bishopbriggs as a commuter village.

52   A group of residents at Brown's Land, about 1920. It was taken a few years before a closure order was issued on the building. Viewing the demolition an aged inhabitant, with tears in her eyes, said 'noo a' are gane, and I think they might have let the auld buildin' stan, for my time won't be long besides, the rent o'the auld house suited my slender purse'. Note the bare feet of the children.

53 This photograph shows a group of residents, mainly children, of the houses known as 'The Diggings'. They comprised two rows of houses called Ure's Land and Brown's Land, and dated from before 1857. In 1928 they had reached such a bad state of repair that a closing order was placed on Brown's Land. The houses were accessed from the main road by an alleyway. The site is now occupied by the Triangle Shopping Centre car park.

54   In this scene we have a 'lighter' drawn by two horses, approaching Cadder from the east. Horse power along the canal was necessarily a slow process. As traffic increased the problem became worse, even after the introduction of steam-driven transport. The vessel shown here was used to carry a variety of cargoes, including iron ore, coal, sand and timber. Some local farms used this type of transport to carry agricultural produce and equipment to other farms and markets.

55   This is an illustration of Cadder Church, from a postcard postmarked 1902. Cadder Church is situated beside a small wood adjoining the canal. A church has stood on or near this site since 1150. The present church was completed in 1829, and renovated in 1908. In the kirkyard many of the stones date back to the first half of the seventeenth century. There is a small stone building in the centre of the kirkyard, where in earlier days watchers took turns on duty to protect the dead from the bodysnatchers. Outside this building there is a seven foot iron coffin made of metal half an inch thick. It was intended for placing over a coffin inside the grave, so preventing interference with the dead.

56   Here we have a Sunday School trip, about to depart, at Cadder Church Hall on Kirkintilloch Road. Cadder Church now has two halls. The north hall was previously Cadder School and the south hall, which we see here, was built in 1896. The church members called for a hall to be built within the village to enable the work of the church to reach the centre of population. The building, ecclesiastical in design, was erected and fully furnished at a cost of around £1,300. It was intended that the hall be used for evening services, bible classes, sunday schools etc. Nowadays the hall is a centre of community activity within the village.

57 This haymaking scene was photographed at Robroyston Farm in 1920. Robroyston was just one of the many farms which bordered Bishopbriggs and Auchinairn. Agriculture played an important part in the economic and social life of the area. This labour intensive method of haymaking was a common site in the fields around Bishopbriggs up until the 1950s. The farm is now derelict.

58   This photograph of Auchinairn Brass Band was taken at the unveiling of the Wallace Monument at Robroyston, on 4 August 1900. The band would certainly have added to the spectacle with their fine uniforms and gleaming instruments. There is little information about the early days of the band. They came into existence sometime before 1890, and it has been said that they used to have a band shed behind the present Auchinairn Tavern. According to contemporary newspaper reports they were often in demand for concerts and other civic functions.

59   Auchinairn House was situated to the south of Old Auchinairn village. The house commanded a fine view at the top of the hill, opposite The Groves, and had imposing entrance gates on the roadway. In the middle of the eighteenth century Dr. William Leechman, Principal of Glasgow University, occupied the estate and house at Auchinairn. In the mid-nineteenth century the house was taken over by Thomas Leslie and became known as 'Leslie's'.

60   This building, on Auchinairn Main Street, was known as 'Paddy's Castle'. The photograph was taken at the time of its demolition in the 1920s. It was used as a lodging house for Irish railway workers during the nineteenth century – hence the name. There were many immigrant Irish labourers in the area at that time for the construction of the Edinburgh to Glasgow Line. There was also an infamous murder associated with this building. In 1840 two navvies murdered a railway foreman, John Green, at Crosshill and were hanged at Bearyards Farm. The two navvies, Dennis Doolan and Patrick Redding, lived here at 'Paddy's Castle'.

61 Old Auchinairn, or the 'Auld Toun', is in fact the original village. Some lock-up garages now stand on the site. The old village has a long history and Roy's map of the area (1755) has Auchinairn as the most prominent village in the locality. In the early years of the nineteenth century the village was inhabited mainly by cotton handloom weavers and afterwards by railway workers and miners. The row of houses in the photograph is known as 'The Tombs'. It seems that when cholera broke out early in the last century the victims were buried on this site. The old village faded into obscurity with the expansion of 'new' Auchinairn in the twentieth century.

62 The village of Auchi-nairn really only consisted of one street – the Main Street. The history of the new village began with the making of the canal and the new Inchbelly turnpike during the eighteenth century. The village was founded by weavers, who were replaced by quarrymen, locomotive workers and miners. 'Paddy's Castle' is situated on the left side of the street, and the houses adjacent were typical weavers' cottages.

63 Another view of Auchinairn Main Street, taken around the turn of the century. If you stand on the Main Street today, just next to the war memorial, it is possible to identify the location of some of these buildings. On the left the sandstone villa and the small white-washed house (No. 186) are still there, while further down the street 'Shoprite' now stands on the site. On the right the first house is still there, while the large sandstone building adjacent to it is now Auchinairn Community Centre.

64   This is a photograph of Jean Letham milking a cow at Auchinairn Farm in 1918. In the nineteenth and early twentieth centuries dairy farming was a principal occupation in the district. The *New Statistical Account*, in 1842, stated that 'almost every farmer has a churning as well as a thrashing machine, all driven by horse power; and the quantity of milk that is taken to Glasgow, sweet and sour, every day, is almost incredible'. This photograph is particularly interesting because it shows a natural pose for the milkmaid, who appears to have dispensed with the milking stool. Many photographs of milkmaids are 'studio shots' of them posing with their pail and stool.

65　This is Cadder Parish Church Manse, which was situated on the canal side at Cadder. It existed there until the Second World War, when the extraction of sand at the nearby quarry necessitated its removal. A new Manse was established in Balmuildy Road when the Rev. J. Gordon took over in 1942.

66   This is the tenement row at Colston, pictured in the early 1900s. Colston marked the boundary between Springburn and Bishopbriggs, and in the early years of this century a large part of it became integrated into the Bishopbriggs area. This photograph shows an interesting array of tenement styles shortly after they were built in 1900. They were occupied mainly by railway workers, quarrymen and miners.

COLSTON, NEAR BISHOPBRIGGS

67   This postcard of Kenmure Avenue, looking towards the Cross, shows a rather different view than that of more recent times. The mature trees to the left and right create a leafy calm, which contrasts with the busy scenes at the Cross today. Through the trees to the right we can glimpse the railway station. The trees have now gone; the Cross Court shopping precinct was erected to the right of the picture in the early 1970s.

Bishopbriggs

68 A later view of Bishop-briggs Cross, just after the Second World War. The main change in this picture is the removal of the tram terminus from Kirkintilloch Road to Kenmure Avenue on the left. There had been discussions regarding the re-siting of the terminus as early as 1914. Work finally commenced on the project in 1940.

Bishopbriggs.
Lanarkshire.

69   This postcard gives a clear view of tenements along Kirkintilloch Road, just north of the Cross. The postcard is dated 1907 and shows an interesting selection of shops and businesses along the street. Judging from the group of children gathered in the street the taking of this picture was quite an event. An open-topped tramcar waits at the terminus in the background.

70 This photograph shows Kirkintilloch Road looking south, about 1900. It gives a good view of the area now occupied by the Triangle Shopping Centre. The chimney on the left belonged to Kemp's joinery works and sawmill. Further along we can see the buildings which were shown as Schoolfield. It was not until the turn of the century that the right side of the road was developed, and here we can still see the boundary wall of Kenmure Estate. The early village was very much a one-sided affair.

71   The Crow Tavern is first shown on maps of this area in 1896. The tavern was remodelled in 1902-1903 by Alexander McDonald of the Glasgow Firm of McDonald and Currie, and later alterations were carried out in 1953. This is a typical business or trade picture of an establishment, with the staff and customers posing outside the building. The tall box on the wall, underneath the street number, dates from the time of the trams. This 'Bundy' was used by the tram driver to punch his time card.

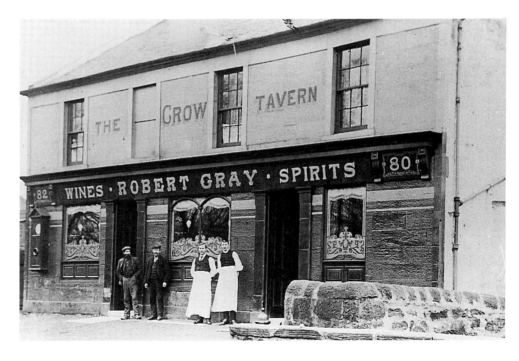

72   Tennent, the licensed grocer, stood next to Quin's public house in the first half of this century. The shop was run by Davy Johnston, and he may well have been present in this formal staff photograph taken outside the shop. There was a pend next to the shop which led to a back court in which a large villa stood, reputedly built for the original owner Mr. Tennent. Note the fine overalls and tidy window display.

73 This is a view of the police and fire station in Kirkintilloch Road, sometime in the 1920s. This county building was erected in 1915. The police station still occupies this site while the fire station has moved on to larger premises in Hilton Road. In the background we can see the hose-drying tower used by the fire brigade.

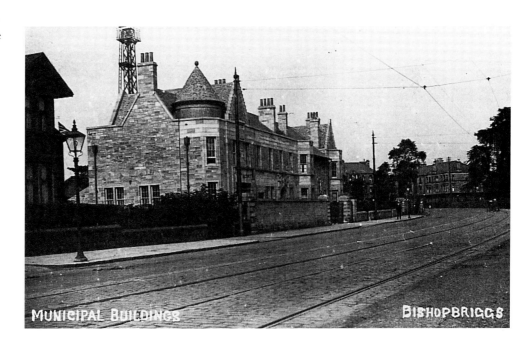

74 Wallace's Well at Robroyston was a popular walk from Bishopbriggs in the first half of this century. The distance was two-and-a-half miles. The well contains a permanent supply of pure water and William Wallace is thought to have sampled the well water while in hiding at Robroyston. The well is situated about half a mile from the monument heading towards Easter Lumloch.

75 Cawder House Curling Club was set up in 1894, although there had been a curling club in Cadder since the early nineteenth century. The pond used here was situated close to the entrance to the grounds of Cadder House. Curling was in the beginning essentially a country game and was popular with farmers. In the eighteenth and nineteenth centuries good curling ponds were abundant, because low-lying areas were open to the elements and low ground was often too wet to bear crops.

76   This photograph was taken on Kenmure Farm in 1935, and shows farm worker Fred Jordan with a team of Clydesdale horses. These horses were a familiar sight around Bishopbriggs and it was not until the 1940s that tractors began to oust the working horse. The switch to tractors was gradual and many farms continued to use both until well after the Second World War.